The Lighter Side of Bomb Disposal

by Richard Ruef

Illustrated by Jonathan Brown

Dorrance Publishing Co
585 Alpha Drive
Suite 103
Pittsburgh, PA 15238
Visit our website at *www.dorrancebookstore.com*

ISBN: 979-8-89499-013-2
eISBN: 979-8-89499-512-0

The Shoebox

When I was in the Army, I was an Explosive Ordnance Disposal Specialist.

In the U.S. Army, Explosive Ordnance Disposal (EOD) is a subset of the Ordnance Corps, and its assigned task is the disarmament of bombs, cannon shells, improvised explosive devices (homemade devices), chemical weapons, and anything else that's explosive—from unfired bullets to flares to hand grenades to nuclear weapons.

Every U.S. armed service has EOD teams; they're even on ships. In the U.S., it's volunteer work with extensive and expensive training, so it's something one must want to do. Some other countries actually order their soldiers and sailors to take on jobs like EOD, but in my case, it wouldn't have mattered since I wanted to do it anyway.

EOD detachments are spotted all over the country on various armed forces posts and bases. The one I was assigned to was a small Army post in the middle of farm country near the Atlantic coast. The next closest EOD detachment was on a large Army training post about forty or fifty miles away, but their detachment was mostly dedicated to that post and didn't often go out on civilian calls the way we did.

Some notes about the team I was on:

Captain Davis was about a dozen years older than I was and went into the Army straight from college. His degree was in Business Management, and he was a pretty decent guy. He lived with his wife and young daughter in officers' housing off-post. He stuck with officers when he was off duty but was friendly, though proper, and professional with us when he was on duty (except for office pranks). He knew the job well and had risen through the officer ranks to captain pretty quickly for a guy who hadn't seen combat.

First Sergeant Hemmings had been in the Army and EOD for dog's ages, was also married and had two grown children, one of each gender, who lived in other states, and one grandchild, a boy, who was his daughter's. He was slightly aloof towards me when I first met him, having been in the Army longer than I had been alive, but loosened up after we had worked together on a few incidents and he saw that I knew what I was doing. He had seen combat, and when he wore his Class A uniform he had a whole bowl of fruit salad on his chest. When I left the Army, Captain Davis told me that it had been Hemmings who had approached him with the idea of getting me a Commanding General's Commendation.

Staff Sergeant Wilson had a German wife with whom he lived off-post and with whom he argued constantly about moving back to Germany. He had met her when he had been stationed there. With everyone else he got along great, but she, he once told me, had gotten the idea that moving away from her home wasn't her favorite plan and it was his fault. He, of course, had no choice in the matter, being in the Army and having to go where he was told. She once came into the office to squawk at him, but interestingly enough she kissed him on the way out, so go figure. He was a guy who knew his stuff forward and backward, having enlisted specifically for EOD way back when.

I was Specialist 4 Richard Ruef, which used to be called a Tech Corporal in my father's day, one notch above a Private First Class. I was new to the EOD game. I started out in the infantry but was able to take a test for non-officer specialties training and, even though EOD wasn't on the list of options, I, being a wise guy, wrote it in on the bottom margin of the sheet, and, wow, I was accepted! I was the lowest-ranking member of the team, not counting John, our civilian clerk, who didn't go out on calls with us. The rest of the team usually called me "Rufus."

One day we were sitting around in the kitchen of our office/barracks building shooting the breeze. We were talking about tricks we had played on each other and mistakes we had made, which determined who had to buy the beer for afterhours, supplied by the one of us who had screwed up most recently.

On that particular day I had that honor.

Two days ago, I had attempted to blow up a live souvenir hand grenade that a police department had received from a WWII vet who decided he didn't need it in his attic anymore. However, EOD people work in pairs or more and I hadn't noticed that my partner had spit into the open end of my blasting cap, which stopped the fuse from burning beyond that point, and in turn kept the cap from exploding and setting off the plastic explosive I had placed on top of the grenade to destroy it. I hadn't looked into the cap before I pushed the tip of the fuse into it, and when the shot hadn't gone off, it had cost me two cases of beer.

While we were sitting in the kitchen talking, the phone rang. John, the detachment clerk, took the call. The police department in a town a few miles away had picked up a shoebox left in the doorway of a store and opened it. Inside the shoebox was a metal box, three inches by four and two inches deep, with multiple wires going into a small hole on one end, and the lid held down by four screws, one at each corner.

There was also a handwritten note that said: "Don't cut the wrong wire."

First Sergeant Hemmings and I were on the schedule for calls that day, so he put the toolbox into the two-and-a-half-ton truck while Captain Davis marked us down as

"VOCO," or "Verbal Orders Commanding Officer," on the duty board. I climbed into the driver's side of the truck, while the sergeant took the other seat, and we were on our way. It took us about twenty minutes to get to the town where the action was.

Sometimes municipal or state bomb squads wear protective clothing on calls and padded and/or armored clothing is often worn in combat situations, but domestic EOD teams don't have that kind of clothes and generally just wear either fatigues or, depending on the type of call, Class A greens (like a suit). Chemical weapons disarmament is different; for that we would wear a chemical-proof full-body rubber suit with a hood. This time we wore Class A greens because were interfacing with a police department.

When we found the police station, the desk officer called downstairs to his duty officer, a lieutenant, who came up from the basement and escorted us down to a holding cell where the shoebox was sitting in the middle of the floor.

First Sergeant Hemmings said, "It's all yours, Rufus," and he sat down on the metal bunk inside the cell.

I figured that the police had picked the box up, opened it, driven it around in a patrol car, and put it back down. Nothing bad had happened, so I picked it up and put it on the bunk next to the sergeant.

It didn't look too complicated. The metal box inside the shoebox either held some explosive, some sort of fuse, and a blasting cap, or it was a hoax. The lid of the metal box was held down by four screws, one at each corner. The risks of opening the metal box were the possibilities of a spring-loaded "mousetrap" actuator that could either snap down on a primer cap and set off any explosive or close an electrical circuit and do the same thing. I had a choice: open the box or bring the thing out to the demolition range and blow it up. Actually, there was a third choice, but I didn't think of it at the time.

People who leave real bombs around don't usually leave hints like "Don't cut the wrong wire," so I decided to open the metal box. I got out my screwdriver and my knife and looked at First Sergeant Hemmings.

"Sure," he said. "If you think so."

He was grinning while he said it, so I removed the two screws on one side and levered the lid of the box up about an eighth of an inch with the point of my knife. I took the flashlight out of the toolbox and peered into the box as best as I could. I didn't see anything that looked like a spring or a tensioned wire pressing against the lid from inside, just a half-dozen wires coming in from a hole at the end of the box, and those wires weren't insulated and were touching one another. I saw that there wasn't a battery for power in either the shoebox or the metal box, and the wires were grounded against each other, so I levered the lid up as far as I could and looked again.

I still didn't see anything I didn't want to see, so I lowered the lid; I figured there was no fuse and no explosive,

BANG
YOU
DOPE!
Don't cut the wrong wire.

so the thing was a hoax. I then removed the two screws from the other end of the box and lifted off the lid.

The wires that came into the box didn't attach to anything inside. But there was another note, at the bottom of the box.

It said: "Bang, you dope!"

Once we were on the way back home, First Sergeant Hemmings, staring straight ahead, said, "That's a case of beer, Rufus."

"Why?" I asked, incredulous.

"You should have disarmed it in the parking lot, so if it had been real it wouldn't have taken the whole building with it."

That would have been the third choice that I mentioned a little while back.

"It still would've taken *me* with it!" I yelled.

"True," he replied, "but what's the point of blowing up you *and* the building?"

I fumed all the way back to the post but had no good reply to that.

A Nice Day for a Drive

One day while Captain Davis, Staff Sergeant Wilson and I were sitting in the office and John, the civilian detachment clerk, was away from his desk, the phone rang. I answered the call and passed it to the captain, who spoke briefly before letting the caller know that we'd be there sometime that afternoon. After hanging up, he turned to the two of us and said, "They found more stuff up at the dredging. We'll take a drive up there in the deuce-and-a-half, pick the stuff up, and bring it over to the old coastal fort for disposal, all in one trip."

Next to a river, about an hour's drive from our post, there had been a munitions plant that had exploded during WWII, scattering partially assembled mortar shells and artillery rounds all over the place. The good news was that none of it had fuses, making it a lot safer to dispose of. The bad news was that they were dredging a new, large boat basin in the river and kept bringing up dredging buckets containing highly explosive hardware.

Without fuses the rounds were safe to handle as long as you didn't hit them hard with something like a dredge bucket. The dredging guys had been very careful, digging slowly and cautiously, and so far there hadn't been any accidents. The crew had been placing the stuff out on the riverbank, away from the work area. Whenever they found something, we would drive over there, pick it up, and bring it to some old coastal gun emplacements that were no longer in use. We would destroy it by placing plastic explosives on top of it and blowing it up, or rather, blowing it down, which is safer. This was not only good practice training but also qualified us for our monthly additional hazardous duty pay.

It was easy work as long as you were careful and no one spit into your blasting cap while you weren't looking.

After writing our destinations on the duty board next to our names, the captain loaded two sticks of C-4 plastic explosive into a box and placed it in the back of the two-and-a-half-ton truck. Meanwhile, I cut off six feet of rope-like time delay fuse, and Staff Sergeant Wilson put the blasting cap transport box on the passenger side floor of the truck's cab, as main-charge high explosives and blasting caps are not carried together. The three of us clambered into the front seat, with me, being the lowest-ranking person, taking the driver's seat. We set out, leaving John and First Sergeant Hemmings to mind the phones. It was a nice day, and I took it easy, reaching the dredging site in a little over an hour.

When we arrived, I drove through the gate of the work area and parked next to the trailer that served as the dredging company's on-site office. The foreman came out to meet us and called through the truck's window, "Sorry to bring you fellas all the way out here, but we dug up a pretty good haul this time, and I didn't want it sitting around here any longer than it had to."

"Not a problem," the captain replied. "It's a nice day for a drive, and it's what we get paid for."

"Better you than me," the foreman laughed and waved us around back of the trailer.

I swung the truck around the trailer and across the open field that separated the work area from where the munitions were laid out on the riverbank. I backed up to them and we all climbed out and went around to the back of the truck where, laid out on the ground, we found four mortar rounds and a 105-millimeter cannon round.

"That's a nice haul," the captain remarked. Usually, they had one or maybe two rounds for us.

We dropped the tailgate, and Sergeant Wilson climbed up into the bed of the truck while I carried the munitions over, one at a time, handing them up to the sergeant. He placed them in the front of the truck bed and wedged the sandbags around and on top of them, which we had kept in the truck for that purpose.

"They're not going anywhere," Sergeant Wilson said. "Just don't hit any bumps on the way out of here."

"You don't have to tell me," I said as we climbed back into the cab. I put it in gear and drove slowly across the rough ground out to the road, waving to the foreman as we passed by him.

Once we got on the road, it took another forty minutes to reach the old fort where we were going to destroy the munitions, and I took it easy on this leg of the trip to avoid unnecessarily jostling the munitions. Explosives that have been sitting around in the ground or water for years and then dried out while sitting on a riverbank can become extra sensitive.

The old fort was actually a series of half a dozen cement pits, sunken into the ground along the top of a cliff. It overlooked the ocean, with a dirt road running beneath it for about a mile, reaching the main road. There were two sets of three pits each, which were former shore gun emplacements. These pits were connected by tunnels to each other and to two observation pits situated at the edge of the cliff. The entire area was surrounded by a high chain-link fence topped with razor wire. It was about three hundred yards long and one hundred yards deep. Signs that read DANGER and NO TRESPASSING – U.S. GOVERNMENT lined the fence every twenty feet or so.

The captain unlocked the gate, and I drove us around the perimeter track twice, honking the horn and shouting,

"Hello, hello, is anyone here?" I shouted this a few times; I was looking for kids or anyone who might have been fooling around in there. The entire area was flat, with scrubby little tufts of weeds scattered here and there. No one responded to me.

I backed the deuce-and-a-half up close to one of the pits, and we all got out. Sergeant Wilson carried the box with the blasting caps. He placed the box down about twenty feet away from the edge of the pit and returned to the tail of the truck while I climbed up and handed the munitions down to him one at a time. He carried the rounds down the steps, into the shallow hole in the ground, and laid the shells out next to each other in the center of the empty pit.

Meanwhile, the captain opened the box of C-4, took out a block, unwrapped it, and cut it in half lengthwise with his knife. I cut off a foot of the time delay fuse, set it down on the ground, and lit one end of it with my lighter. It took a little over a minute to burn its way to the other end. "Three minutes for three feet," I announced, as I cut off another two feet of fuse and put it back in the truck. The remaining three feet I gave to Sergeant Wilson, who took it over to the blasting cap box. Removing a cap from the box, he squinted while looking into the open end. Satisfied with what he saw—or didn't see—he pushed the tip of the fuse into the blasting cap. Facing us, he used his crimping tool to crimp the end of the cap to the fuse behind his back. After putting the cap and fuse down, he went back down into the pit.

Captain Davis brought the C-4 half-blocks over to the sergeant, who put them down in a line on top of the shells. He kneaded their ends together, forming one long block of plastic explosive. Then, he pushed the pointed end of his crimping tool's handle into the middle of the long block of C-4, creating a hole about an inch deep.

The captain carried the cap and fuse over to the pit, gave it to the sergeant, and joined me in the truck.

Sergeant Wilson took the blasting cap and fuse over to the plastic explosive, pushed the cap into the hole he had made in the C-4, attached an igniter to the other end of the fuse, and yelled, "Ready!"

I started the truck (because it's always nice to make sure your escape method works before you need it) and gave three good blasts on the horn. Sergeant Wilson yelled, "Fire in the hole!" three times, pulled the ring on the igniter, lit the fuse, and then quickly and carefully walked up the steps out of the pit and got in the truck.

I drove about two hundred yards or so, turned the truck sideways to the pit, and we got out. Standing with the truck between us and the pit, we waited, seemingly forever, for the blast.

When the blast finally came, it was immediately followed by a huge eruption less than twenty feet from us—hundreds of dark, jagged objects shot into the air.

Brown
inkstains.com

"Frag!" the captain yelled, and he and I dove our heads under the truck. "Frag" being short for "fragmentation," which refers to the pieces of what you're blowing up that get tossed into the air by the blast and can fall back down on you.

Frag? That didn't make any sense. I didn't hear any metal pieces falling on or around the truck, and Sergeant Wilson was still standing calmly next to the truck.

"Connecting tunnel ventilation shaft," the sergeant said. "You gentlemen can come out now."

It had been leaves. A century's worth of fallen leaves had erupted from a nearby ventilation air shaft. I felt a bit foolish as I brushed myself off, and a glance at the captain showed that he felt silly, too.

Sergeant Wilson had a wide grin on his face. "Begging your pardon, Captain, but I believe that's a couple of cases of beer from each of you."

TWO cases each, I thought to myself. That was coming it a bit strong, I felt, and I was getting tired of having to spend some of my hard-earned pay this way, but the boss was going along with the penalty so I couldn't very well argue.

To show him he WAS the boss, Captain Davis made Sergeant Wilson drive on the way home, but the sergeant had been right; I guess we deserved the penalty, and on the way, we stopped at the Post Exchange and bought the four cases of beer, paying for two each.

Carrying On

Our Army Explosive Ordnance Disposal detachment had a rather large latrine. That's because our building had been a forty-man barracks, but now housed just me—during the night. In the daytime, there were five of us: Captain Davis, First Sergeant Hemmings, Staff Sergeant Wilson, our civilian clerk John and, of course, yours truly.

And it was a bright yellow latrine. Including the ceiling. Which is a somewhat involved story, and here it is:

We dismantled, or more often destroyed, bombs, cannon shells, hand grenades, and the like, and surprisingly frequently war souvenirs that ex-GIs no longer wanted kicking around in their attics, basements, or dens. In fact, every couple of months or so, some police department or an ex-GI himself (it's always a "him") called us with some sort of prize brought back from overseas that was no longer wanted. Usually, it was the "her" that lived with the "him" who wanted the item gotten rid of, and we always obliged. After all, that's the sort of thing we were there for.

Usually, it was small stuff—grenades, twenty-millimeter anti-aircraft (AA) rounds, a pretty good quantity of fifty-caliber bullets, stuff like that. We used the .50 caliber. However, twenty-millimeter AA shells and grenades are a little dicey, so we took them off-post and destroyed them by blowing them up.

We crafted pen and pencil sets with the .50 cal. or made desk nameplates, which we traded around post for beer, cold cuts, pastry, and the like—all on the QT, you understand. All in all, it was a pretty good racket and gave us something to do between callouts.

With the .50 cal., we separated the bullet nose from the brass propellant-filled shell, dumped out the propellant powder, put the brass with its primer in a vise, and scared the heck out of the Red Cross office in the next building by tapping the primer with a hammer and nail. If the round was electrically fired, we used a battery to fire it. It went off like a .22 or a large firecracker.

The items now deemed safe, we reassembled the two pieces and epoxied them, base down, to a very nice-looking finished board that we got by trading the completed product with the post's carpenter shop.

We ordered the pens and pencils by mail, while the nameplates we obtained from a local jeweler. The jeweler would then engrave them on fancy brass plaques that we had sourced from the metalsmithing shop on-post. None of this cost us too much; we all chipped in, and of course, we all shared in the goodies we traded for.

Anyway, one day, First Sergeant Hemmings, who was our very own Sergeant Bilko, traded a nice pen and pencil set to the post's paint shop for a five-gallon can of bright, school bus yellow paint.

"What in hell are you planning on doing with that?" asked the captain.

"Rufus can paint the ceiling of the latrine," replied the sergeant.

"Yellow?"

"They were out of white."

Now, I guess I should explain why the latrine ceiling needed painting. A couple of weeks earlier, a local school janitor had acquired (taken without permission) a jar of small pieces of sodium metal in oil from the science lab of the school where he worked. He had decided that the way to clean the school's drains was to toss a chunk of sodium down them. This had been a spectacularly bad idea. Sodium, in the presence of water, explodes. In fact, it's so antsy that if you leave it out of its usual oil bath, it spontaneously catches fire just from the moisture in the air. But this wizard thought it would just burn in the drains and clear out the hairballs and grease.

This sort of thing happened frequently. If it wasn't souvenir hand grenades or artillery shells, it was signal flares and things like that.

Fortunately, he ran his great idea by his buddy first, who strongly suggested he call the fire department and ask them to take the jar off his hands. Knowing what it could do, the fire department called us. Heaven knows why he didn't just sneak the stuff back to where he had gotten it from, but maybe he figured sneaking it out was chancy enough.

The fire department sent two guys over with the jar, and I asked them if they would like a demonstration of what happens when you put sodium into water. They, being as foolish as I now admit I had been, said yes.

Since it was raining out, I didn't want to pull a piece of sodium out of its oil outside. So, I half filled a bucket with water in the latrine, used tweezers to take a quarter-inch cube of the metal from the jar, and tossed it into the water.

The firefighters and I were really quite impressed.

So was First Sergeant Hemmings the next day when he saw the hundreds of little burn marks speckled all over the ceiling. He wasn't very happy. He had been in the Army longer than I'd been alive and took a dim view of lower-ranking soldiers doing stupid things they should have known better than to do. He fined me two cases of beer and told me to paint the ceiling with the yellow paint.

The captain wasn't too thrilled about it, either. "Painting the ceiling's not punishment enough. Besides, the rest of the latrine is pretty dingy. Rufus, paint the whole thing, and make it three cases of beer."

And that explains how we ended up with a bright yellow latrine.

One other thing about the place: when they converted the barracks into our office, they stripped everything out of the latrine except three commodes and three sinks. In the corner, they installed a one-man shower stall, replacing the half-room affair that had originally been there.

So, one morning, I was in this big, empty, bright yellow room shaving; it was around ten o'clock (hey, I had been called out late the night before) when the latrine door opened.

I glanced up in the mirror (because you never knew if someone was about to toss in firecrackers or a smoke grenade, or who knows what). To my surprise, the post commander—a two-star general—stood in the doorway with his mouth hanging open. His gaze fixed upon the vast latrine that had been painted bright yellow, including the ceiling, a space that contained me—a GI in his skivvies, shaving at ten o'clock in the morning.

The only time I had ever seen him before was when blank-firing cannons had been shot off on-post to honor a VIP, and EOD had been there in case something went wrong. Fortunately, back then, nothing did. It sure looked like something was going to go wrong for me this time, though.

I dropped the razor into the sink, spun around, and came to attention. He slowly surveyed the room, shook his head, and said, "Carry on." He glanced around once more, turned, and left.

Braez
INKSTAINS.COM

I imagine he figured that the peculiar situation was beyond his pay grade, or perhaps he thought EOD guys were as nutty as the rumors had alluded. Fortunately, we never encountered him again. It was also fortunate that, seemingly, the general had a short memory, or a forgiving nature. When I left the Army, he presented me with—via my captain—a fancy Commanding General's Commendation, a certificate suitable for framing. That was nice. I had it for years before it disappeared sometime during a move. I suppose I did deserve the honor. I was good at my job, but it was the things I got involved in that *weren't* in my job description that got me in trouble—like almost burning down the building by nearly lighting the latrine on fire!

Pole Vaulting

One fall morning, bright and early, Captain Davis breezed into our US Army Explosive Ordnance Disposal detachment office, brimming with a great idea.

"Rufus," he said, "how'd you like to blow up a Navy base?"

"Sure, Captain!" I replied. "But isn't the closest base around here the one with our demolition range? I mean, well, we blow that up all the time."

"Well, yes, but this time we're invited onto the base itself." He called First Sergeant Hemmings and me into his office and explained, "The Navy wants us to take down a tall signal pole that's no longer in use. It's up on a cliff overlooking a beach that's used by the base's sailors and their families during the summer. The pole is old and starting to lean. And it's rusty."

As the story unfolded, it appeared that the previous night, the Navy lieutenant commander who oversaw the grounds at the base and Captain Davis had been at our post's Officers' Club and had decided that the best way to take the pole down was to blow it up—or, rather, to explosively cut it off at the bottom. We may assume that a few drinks had influenced in this decision.

In all fairness, the idea had some merit: cutting it off a couple of feet above the ground, nice and clean, aiming for it to fall away from the cliff...should be a snap. I mean, explosive cutting is used all the time in demolition, and our detachment was the closest bunch of demolition guys around. And we never passed up a chance to blow something up.

We talked it over, and the captain, along with his Navy buddy, decided to have the beach closed off for us at the time of the demolition. Despite the chill of late fall, there was a concern that someone might go walking on it if not deterred.

A week later, with the beach deserted, and the Shore Patrol ensuring the area around the pole was clear of anyone who wasn't in our party, we found ourselves on the cliff above the beach with the lieutenant commander and a couple of ensigns, gathered around the object of interest. In the clear, cool (sober) light of day, the lieutenant commander, who outranked our captain by a grade, was a little skeptical.

"Captain, are you quite sure this is going to work?" he asked, somewhat dubiously.

Captain Davis, amidst all of us lowlifes, was very military and formal. He replied, "Yes, sir, it should go very easily, sir. We'll just cut it off at the base and drop it onto the grass here."

"All right, then, go ahead. How far back do you want us, Captain?"

"On the other side of the fence there, should be far enough, sir. The beach is blocked off?"

"Yes, sir, it is," replied an ensign, saying "sir" because an Army captain is two grades above an ensign but three below a Navy captain. In Navy ranks, a captain ranks like one of our colonels, unless in charge of a boat. If the boat is small enough, our captain could outrank their captain, who might not actually be a captain but is called that anyway. This is because the captain of a boat, regardless of actual rank, is always the boss when on board. Navy ranks are weird.

Once the Navy was safely out of the picture, Captain Davis looped a piece of quarter-inch clothesline around the pole about three feet off the ground and taped it to the pole. Then, he and First Sergeant Hemmings packed one and a half pounds of C-4 plastic explosive on top of the clothesline, creating a shaped charge around the pole. The way this works is based on the fact that explosive force leaves the explosive perpendicular to the explosive's surface. By placing the plastic explosive on top of the clothesline they formed a "tunnel" in the C-4, because clothesline provides so little resistance to the explosive force of C-4 that it's as if the clothesline isn't even there. While the force of the explosion goes outward, away from the outer surface, it also goes inward, converging and concentrating at the center bottom of the "tunnel." This concentration of force along a thin line around the pole effectively cuts through the metal.

Once they had the shaped charge set up, they taped another half-pound of C-4 to the pole. It was placed as high as First Sergeant Hemmings could reach, on the side facing the beach, with the intention of pushing the falling pole away from the cliff and onto the grass. Unfortunately, this turned out to be a bad idea.

While that was going on, I ran a spool of double electrical wire out to the fence, about a hundred and fifty yards away, using up almost all the wire, and then waited for the rest of the crew. I could just make out what they were doing in the distance. First Sergeant Hemmings attached an electric blasting cap to the wires and poked a length of explosive detonating cord into the two mounds of plastic explosive, connecting them. He made a hole in the lower mound with the handle of his crimpers and pushed the blasting cap into it. After checking everything, they walked over to the fence where the rest of us were waiting.

I had placed the firing box and its handle about three feet apart on the ground. When the two of them joined us, I connected the two wires to the box, and the captain declared in a loud voice, "I am the Safety Officer!"

I gave the handle to the captain and announced, "The Safety Officer has the handle!" I then passed the hellbox to First Sergeant Hemmings. He took the handle from the captain and said in a loud voice, "The Firing Officer has the handle!" After yelling "Fire in the hole!" three times, he popped the handle into the socket in the box and turned it.

There was the expected double blast, one on top of the other, but since most of the pole's weight was above the upper mound of C-4, the upper blast had kicked only the *bottom* of the pole toward the grass. The remaining hundred-foot-long pole, swung *outward*, teetered on the lip of the cliff for a couple of seconds and, with its top tilted down and bottom aiming toward the sky, it vanished like the mast of a sinking ship over the cliff.

Our group was quiet until First Sergeant Hemmings gave the handle back to Captain Davis and said in a low voice, "The Safety Officer has the handle." The Navy crew came running over, and we all went to the edge of the cliff and looked down. About ninety feet of the iron pole was sticking up in the sand, leaning over at a sharp angle.

The lieutenant commander was laughing uproariously, the two ensigns were grinning from ear to ear, and Captain Davis looked like he wanted to step off the cliff.

"We can put a line on it and pull it down; that doesn't look too hard," the lieutenant commander said, still laughing. "We can cut it up just as easily on the beach as up here. We better do that right away, before it falls over on someone."

"It was a good try," the lieutenant commander told Captain Davis, as he and the ensigns got into their car to

EOD
EOD
Brauz
INKSTAINS.COM

see about taking care of the pole. "And it is down, so that much is a success."

After returning to the post, the captain told me to pull into the Post Exchange. "How many do you think, Sergeant?" the captain asked Hemmings.

"For you, sir? Oh, three cases ought to do it," the sergeant replied with a straight face.

Proof

One wintry day, we received a call from a nearby police department. They had confiscated a foreign concussion grenade and needed evidence that could be used in court to prove that it was a dangerous explosive. They suggested that if we set it off in our explosive's disposal area with both their officers and us as witnesses, it would provide the necessary proof.

Now, a concussion grenade, when it detonates, produces little or no fragmentation. It's employed offensively when its user is out in the open and charging a fortified position. The idea is that, without cover to hide behind, its user can't effectively use a fragmentation grenade. Instead, they aim to throw the concussion grenade close to the enemy, relying on the force of the explosion alone to inflict damage.

We set up a meeting at our office for a couple of days later, and they brought the item with them.

It was quite old and not very complicated—just a plastic bag the size of a baseball, filled with powder. It had a wooden disc at the top that held the detonator and time delay, along with a safety pin and handle (or spoon, as it's called).

No biggie for us; we figured one of us could pull the pin and drop it into one of the observation hole bunkers in the old, abandoned shore battery we used as a demolition range, while a couple more of us and the two police officers would witness the underground explosion. The idea was that when the spoon flew off, the standard four-to-seven-second delay would then expire as the grenade was falling into the hole. Then, the grenade would go high order down in the observation bunker—meaning, it would "explode with a bang" underground—and the police would have their proof.

We agreed on a date a few days away. I secured the spoon to the body of the grenade with a rubber band, ensuring that it couldn't get knocked off accidently and allow the grenade to explode. Then, I locked it in my desk.

On the designated day, I placed the grenade in the back of our 6x6 deuce-and-a-half truck and surrounded it with sandbags. Staff Sergeant Wilson joined me in the truck, and we departed for the old fort, with Captain Davis sitting alongside the two policemen in their car, following us.

As we drove through farm country toward the demolition range, we encountered a narrow, winding road. Ahead of us, a farmer on his tractor was moving much slower than

I liked, so I moved over to pass. The farmer started wildly waving his hands and yelling. I couldn't understand him amid the tractor's and the truck's engine noises, but as we approached, I could see the problem: he had a hay rake attached to the tractor stretched out across the opposite lane of the road. I slammed on the brakes and pulled in behind the tractor, while the farmer made "slow down" motions, patting down with his hands in the air next to him. He turned off into a field a little way along. Fortunately, the rest of the trip was uneventful.

When we arrived, the captain unlocked the gate, and I drove around the compound beeping the horn and yelling, "Demolition warning!" and "Is anyone here? Come out if you are!"—just in case someone had climbed over the barbed wire-topped fence to play in the underground tunnels or something. Throughout my time using that range for demolition, nobody was ever inside the fence when we arrived.

Nobody answered, so we parked a few feet from a suitable observation bunker sunk into the top of the cliff, and everyone got out.

The captain motioned me aside and let me know he was displeased with the tractor episode. All I could do was stand at attention and say, "Yes, sir." He could have easily gigged me a couple of cases of beer, so I got off easy.

Staff Sergeant Wilson retrieved the scissors from the toolbox, carried the grenade over to the observation hole, and checked if we were ready. Holding the spoon tightly against the grenade's body, he cut the rubber band, ready for the spoon to fly off as soon as he let go of the grenade. He yelled, "Fire in the hole!" three times, pulled the pin, dropped the grenade into the bunker, and released the spoon.

It didn't explode high order. That was the good thing. The bad thing was that instead of a short delay and a bang deep in the bunker, there was no delay at all, and a low-order fireball shot out of the hole as soon as the spoon flipped off.

The sergeant fell back to the ground, yelling profanity, his hands covering his face. We all rushed over, yelling, "Are you okay? Can you see?" He sat up, taking his hands off his face.

"Yeah, I can see, and hell no, I'm not okay!" he said, getting to his feet.

"Well, you're going to the doctor when we get back to post, and if he says you need to

be checked out by an eye doctor, then you're going to do that too," Captain Davis ordered. "And I've got two pieces of bad news for you while I'm at it: for one thing, you don't have any eyebrows left, and the hair on the front of your head is gone."

"Yeah? And what's the other bad news?" Staff Sergeant Wilson asked the captain.

"You should have turned away from the pit and let go of the grenade's spoon over the pit behind your back," the captain replied, "and that'll cost you three cases of beer, Wilson!"

Brown
INKSTAINS.COM

But it all ended well.

The doctor did order the sergeant to see an off-post eye specialist, an ophthalmologist, and that took a bit of time. We all went with him, being worried for him, but fortunately, he checked out okay.

The captain and one of the cops testified in court a couple of months later that, while the grenade didn't explode, it was certainly a dangerous incendiary device. As a result, the police obtained a conviction on a lesser charge.

And, hey! I didn't have to buy the beer for a few days!

School Day

A call came into the EOD office one winter Monday morning, a few minutes past seven. A nearby police department wanted us to check out a school that had received a bomb threat. I informed our detachment commander, Captain Davis, and took down the particulars. The captain took the phone, asked a couple of questions, and assured them we'd be there as soon as we could.

We found Staff Sergeant Wilson in the kitchen and briefed him on the situation, as it was his duty turn along with mine. "Well, Rufus," he said to me, "I guess it's back to school for us, huh? Fine way to start the week."

Since the truck was fueled up—that being the last thing we always did before coming back to the office—we grabbed the toolbox, signed out on the duty board and left the captain and First Sergeant Hemmings to hold down the fort (John, our civilian clerk, was not in yet).

It was cold but bright, and it had snowed the night before. "Nice day for skiing," the sergeant remarked as I turned the deuce-and-a-half onto the state highway. "Which is probably why the school got a bomb call this morning."

"Ya think so?"

"Yeah, some kid wanted the day off school," he replied.

We brooded on that for a while, and after a couple of minutes he said, "Never would have tried that when I was a kid. Would have been too scared of getting caught."

I agreed.

The drive wasn't too bad. The state road had been well plowed, and the hills had also been sanded. After about forty-five minutes, we reached the town where the school was. This was an era before cell phones and GPS, so we stopped at a gas station and asked for directions. We were told where the school was and headed over.

It was a parochial school, and outside there were only two police cars and a firetruck. I parked the truck, and we approached the main door, which was locked. After I knocked a few times, a middle-aged man let us in. He thanked us for coming, introduced himself as the principal, and told us that it was likely just a prank, but they had to be sure.

The cops and firefighters were already inside, and we introduced ourselves, although we didn't need much of an introduction, what with our Army uniforms. The principal informed us that the police had received the bomb threat around six in the morning and had notified him at home. He explained that the school had a procedure for that sort of thing. He had called six staff members, each responsible for calling students at home to notify them that school had been cancelled for the day. With all seven of them calling, they had reached all two hundred-odd students' homes in time to prevent them from coming in.

The school custodian had given the master keys for all the hall lockers to the police, so we joined them in searching through those while the firefighters checked the building and the grounds. It took four hours to cover the furnace room, all classrooms and their closets, the office, and the lunchroom. Nothing was found in the lockers except books, some dirty sneakers, a few jackets, and a banana skin. I don't know what nonsense was found in the rest of the building, but according to the fire department, there were no explosives.

When we were done, we assured the principal that we hadn't found anything. He said he was glad there was nothing and thanked us, the police, and the firefighters once again. We said that we felt sorry that school had to be cancelled, but he told us it certainly wouldn't happen again.

We asked him why he was so sure, and he said, "This is a private school. There will be mandatory classes for everyone next Saturday."

We decided to stop for lunch on the way home, choosing a diner we had noticed earlier along the state highway.

Brown
INKSTAINS.COM

We ordered drinks while we checked out the menu. It was an extensive menu and we sat there for a while, me sipping my iced tea and Wilson sucking on his Coke. When the waitress returned for the second time to ask if we were ready to order, we decided it was time to make up our minds. I ordered the meatloaf and Staff Sergeant Wilson chose a grilled cheese sandwich.

When she came back with our food, she observed the badges on our shirts, then shifted her gaze to the parking lot and asked why we paratroopers had red-painted fenders on our truck. Wilson told her to take a closer look at the badges. Startled, she exclaimed, "You're not Airborne! Those are BOMBS on your shirts!" I told her she was right and explained about EOD, and that all EOD vehicles had red fenders. She was suitably impressed.

Then she wanted to know where the bomb was, and Staff Sergeant Wilson told her that there was no bomb, but that we were "just passing through." We shared a few examples of what Explosive Ordnance Disposal does, mentioning that we handled both military and civilian explosive items without disclosing *how* we disarmed military items— those details are secret. Then she had to get back to work. We finished our meal and left her a nice tip to uphold EOD's reputation.

While driving back to post, I told Staff Sergeant Wilson that I guessed there were some schools in which calling in a bomb threat was still a bad idea. He agreed.

The Handle

Explosive Ordnance Disposal training was interesting but at times sort of stressful, kind of like the job itself once we graduated. To let off steam we would play volleyball. The three squads that were in my training class competed against each other as three volleyball teams. When we did demolition training two teams were playing volleyball at any given time while the third team was being trained.

One day, we were out on the demolition range practicing our skills at blowing stuff up while keeping our fingers and eyebrows intact. My friend Binder and I were setting up a shot to be fired off electrically using a detonator box—the kind with a hand crank. When turned, it generates a small current through the wires, setting off the blasting cap and triggering the main charge.

There's a whole formal procedure to follow for this sort of thing and being in training and under the eyes of our instructors, we followed it. We twisted one end of a pair of wires together to prevent a circuit from becoming static electricity. Then we connected the other ends to the electric blasting cap. Binder pushed a hole in the end of a half-pound block of C-4 plastic explosive with the pointed handle of his crimpers, and I pushed the blasting cap into the hole.

As part of our training, we were simulating blowing up, or rather, blowing down, an unexploded bomb or shell. All we had to do was set off the block of C-4 and pretend it was placed on top of the imaginary ordnance that we were trying to get rid of.

Once we had the blasting cap and main charge ready, we unrolled enough wire to get us safely inside "the tank"—a thick-walled repurposed old oil tank lying on its side with a safety glass window cut into one end and a doorway cut in the end away from down range.

Our instructor, a senior sergeant who had been in grade longer than we'd been alive, was waiting for us and had been watching through the window. He was the safety officer for our shot and had the detonator box ready for us. We went through the safety procedure prior to firing the shot. He removed the handle from the box and handed the box to Binder. I untwisted the wires and connected them to the terminals on top of the box.

The sergeant called out in a loud voice, "The Safety Officer has the handle!" He then gave the handle to Binder, who called out just as loud, "The Firing Officer has the handle!" He then yelled, "Fire in the hole!" three times and put the handle into the top of the hellbox and cranked it.

The shot went off perfectly.

Binder gave the handle back to the sergeant who yelled, "The Safety Officer has the handle!" I took the box from Binder, disconnected the wires, and gave the box to the sergeant. We stood down from the procedure and went down range to check things out. It looked good; there was nothing left. The three of us walked back to the field office building a couple of hundred yards or so back from the range and the sergeant reported to the captain that we had done well and had performed the procedure properly.

The captain checked us off on his clipboard and dismissed us, while the next two trainees went with the sergeant down to the range for their turn. We went around to the back of the field office where the volleyball court and the rest of our squads were. We watched the game until it was over and went in to play with the rest of our team for the following game.

We played for a few minutes, and then someone suggested we compete for a couple of cases of beer. Everyone agreed and we started playing in earnest. Whichever team racked up seven points first would win the game. It didn't take long for the score to be tied at six apiece and we really buckled down to it. One of the other squad's players spiked the ball down over the net, but one of our guys was right

inkstains.com

under it for the save and was ready to pop it up for my team to spike it right back down at the other guys.

And then someone on the other team screamed out, "I have the Safety Officer BY THE HANDLE!!!" Both teams burst out laughing uproariously.

Our guy didn't have a chance to make the save, he was laughing so hard.

That evening, our team, of course, bought the beer for the guys who had bested us. As for the third team—the one being trained while we were playing—*they* had to buy their own darn beer!

The Beer Can Stunt

Our Explosive Ordnance Disposal detachment wasn't all work. Sometimes we had fun, though at each other's expense. Even Captain Davis got involved in our (mostly) harmless pranks. Here are a couple of examples:

One afternoon, Captain Davis and First Sergeant Hemmings had been left in the barracks office while the other two of us were out on a call and decided to play a trick on us. Naturally, it was an explosive trick. They dismissed our unit clerk, John, for the day to avoid involving him in the scheme.

The two of them got out a small explosive primer with about the power of a .22 short blank cartridge, called a base coupling. They broke off its plastic covering with pliers and mounted it onto a snap-pressure-release fuse, a mousetrap—both of which we kept in stock for training purposes. They set it up in the refrigerator, placing it behind a can of beer so that any movement of the can would release the

Beer
Brown
inkstains.com

mousetrap's spring, striking the base coupling and setting it off with a loud bang, like a firecracker. They made sure it pointed away from the beer can toward the rear of the refrigerator.

So far, so good. All they had to do was wait for Staff Sergeant Wilson and me to return from our call and go into the fridge for a beer. Then, the prank would take place, costing whichever of us was the victim a case of beer for allowing themselves to be "blown up."

It worked like a charm. We returned to the office later that afternoon, and after the captain received our report, we went into the kitchen to relax. Staff Sergeant Wilson reached into the fridge for a beer, naturally choosing the one closest to the front, and as planned, that was the booby-trapped one, which went off with a BANG!

The sergeant was livid and made it known, especially to First Sergeant Hemmings, whom he blamed for the prank. Then the captain revealed that it had been his idea, and they had both worked on setting it up. Well, Staff Sergeant Wilson couldn't curse out the captain and finally had to admit that it was worth a case of beer. For the next three weeks, he was very leery about picking things up and checked them all carefully first.

The Lightbulb Caper

Staff Sergeant Wilson bought his case of beer like a good sport whenever he was pranked and, in turn, pranked the rest of us when he could. This time he aimed to get even with Captain Davis. Waiting until the captain was out, he replaced the bulb in the captain's wall-mounted light with a red one and wired the lamp to turn on when the captain sat in his chair. It wasn't too difficult to arrange—just a couple of wires separated with a matchstick placed under the chair cushion so they would touch and complete an electrical circuit when the captain sat down. Of course, the scheme involved cutting and splicing the electrical cord that powered the lamp from the wall socket behind the chair. The chances that the captain would notice it were considerably slim.

The captain returned to the office and sat down in his chair. There was a loud SNAP! and the ceiling lights went

inkstains.

out. The sharp scent of something burning filled the air, and smoke curled up from beneath the chair's cushion.

Captain Davis jumped up, yelling, "What the hell was that?!" He turned around, looked down, and saw the wires snaking up under the chair. His eye followed the wires up the wall to the lamp with the red bulb, and he knew in an instant that it was a booby trap—one that had gone very, very wrong.

When the smoke had cleared, both literally and figuratively, he demanded to know who had set up the trap.

Knowing it was best to get it said and done with right away, Staff Sergeant Wilson 'fessed up. The captain wasn't too hard on the sergeant, but the issue of potentially starting a fire in the chair cushion was addressed sternly.

The contraption was unplugged, the circuit breaker turned back on, and a penalty of rewiring the wall lamp, replacing the seat cushion, and providing two cases of beer was imposed.

There was no argument from Staff Sergeant Wilson.

Popping Off

We were always setting traps for each other at my EOD detachment—explosive ones, certainly. Getting caught by one of them cost the victim a case of beer, of course, and conversely, disarming one before being caught by it cost the trap setter a case of beer, or even more than one case.

The idea behind these little pranks was not only to undergo booby trap training when we disarmed our little "mini bombs" but also to bond us together in a serious yet friendly fashion, because we had to work with each other when it was the real thing.

Some of the traps were complicated, but most were relatively simple. Here's an example of one that was simple:

One fine morning, I planned to "bomb" Staff Sergeant Wilson with some firecrackers while he was in the latrine, where I figured he couldn't easily respond to them. I had picked up the firecrackers in town the day before, and no one in the detachment knew I had them. I was counting on them to really surprise him, popping off while he was sitting there with his trousers down around his ankles.

Then I made a mistake: I decided to make things more complicated. Just for the fun of it, I would play some head games with the good sergeant. The plan was to set up a fake trap so obvious that he would start to dismantle it. At that point, I would toss the firecrackers into the latrine near him while he was busy disarming the trap.

Of course, he wouldn't have his pants down around his ankles in that case. But if I did it right, he'd be facing the wall instead of facing the door, where he could have seen the firecrackers coming.

I wired a pull-trigger device to the flush handle behind the bowl of one of the commodes, set to fire a blank .22-sized detonator called a base coupling. I put an "Out of Order" sign on the other commode. The idea was that he'd see the trap and either use the other commode anyway and disarm the trap after he was done with his business, or disarm the trap first. But I figured, in either case, he'd be unable to resist thwarting whoever had set the trap by disarming it at some point, which would have him facing away from the door of the latrine.

I waited until he went into the latrine for his morning business, counted to five, lit the string of firecrackers, opened the door, tossed them in, and closed the door.

LATRINE
Brollz
inkstains.com
PA-POP!
POP!
PA-POP!
POP!

It would have been perfect except that I hadn't counted on one thing: *he didn't see the trap.*

As soon as he turned around and dropped his trousers, he saw the door opening and the firecrackers being tossed in. He pulled up his pants with one hand, ran over, grabbed the firecracker string with the still-burning fuse with his other hand, ran across the floor, let go of his pants, opened the door, and tossed the firecrackers back out.

That still would have been fine, except for two things: one, I had been standing on the other side of the door, and two, so had been Captain Davis, who was waiting for me to get out of the way so he could enter the latrine.

The firecrackers exploded at the captain's feet. He was not amused. He went into the latrine and closed the door.

Half a minute later, I heard the staff sergeant and the captain laughing behind the door.

That little episode cost me two cases of beer: one because Staff Sergeant Wilson did, in fact, thwart my plan by disarming my commode trap, and the other because my plan backfired, and the captain and I turned out to be the ones who got bombed by the firecrackers.

The Wrong Clerk

There was this one time when we all got together and came up with a scheme to booby-trap John, our civilian office clerk.

He had a wooden tray on his desk that held the work he had to do. We drilled a hole in the desk under the tray, glued a string to the bottom of the tray, and tied it to the trigger loop of a pull-pressure fuse (used for booby traps). This fuse was set up with an explosive base-coupling primer. We moved the tray off-kilter on the desk and taped the pull-pressure fuse to the bottom of the desk. This ensured that the string was taut but not under enough pressure to set the whole thing off. It was a relatively simple trick.

The idea was that John would move the tray to straighten it out, which would then set off the trap.

The trouble arose because John didn't work directly for us; he worked for the Post Civilian Administration, which handled everything related to civilian workers. There were quite a few, including the civilian clerks and the mess hall kitchen staff, for example.

So, when John called in sick to his boss the next morning, a replacement was sent over—a grouchy, stern woman who obviously wouldn't tolerate our kind of nonsense.

We had no warning. First Sergeant Hemmings and Staff Sergeant Wilson were in the office, and I was taking my shower when she showed up. The first thing she did after introducing herself was to straighten out the off-kilter tray. I heard the bang all the way from inside the shower, followed closely by her scream.

That's when the captain arrived.

He was able to calm her down, and the promise of a nice lunch off-post kept her from squealing on us. Meanwhile, I got dried off and dressed. When lunchtime came, the two sergeants took her to lunch while the captain, who wasn't allowed to fraternize with enlisted troops, ate in the Officers' Mess. As the lowest ranking, I held down the fort minding the office phones. But don't worry about me; I ate in the Enlisted Mess when they came back.

By the time she left in the afternoon, we were forgiven. However, at lunch, the sergeants had made a serious mistake by explaining why we had booby-trapped the desk, including the details about the cases of beer.

Once she got the idea of the jokes we played on each other and how beer was an integral part of the shenanigans,

BOOM
IN
OUT

she laughingly told the captain that each of us was penalized two cases of beer, including him.

So, she ended up being a good sport after all, and that evening, after she had gone home, all four of us chipped in for the beer.

Guard Duty

During training, I found myself involved in a number of assignments that had nothing to do with EOD matters—or at least not directly.

On several occasions, I was on night guard duty in our main EOD training building. The Navy ran the school, on an all-services base. Along with a bunch of soldiers in our class, we had a few sailors, a couple of Air Force guys, a Coast Guardsman, and two foreign students.

All of the students, including the foreign students, stood guard duty. Actually, all of us did everything that was to be done, but we never played pranks at the school. I guess it was just too serious a place. The exceptions to this were what happened at the volleyball game that I mentioned above and the canoe trip that my buddy Parch and I took.

Now, you have to remember that all of our training was classified, at least Secret, and although none of the ordnance we trained with inside the school building was dangerous, having all been rendered safe, much of it was lying around or in unlocked cabinets. Some items had been cut open to display their innards so we could understand how they operated, or at least how they were supposed to operate.

All of this had to be kept away from the public to prevent those without the proper security clearance from gaining knowledge about how the stuff worked.

Ever since the building had been used as an EOD school, there had been a nightly guard patrolling the corridors, both upstairs and downstairs, armed with a loaded .45 automatic pistol.

Until, that is, late one night when the guard on duty had fired a round at something that had frightened him, creating a hole in the wall. That incident occurred before my time, and I'm sure glad I wasn't around when it took place. The trouble that guard had caused must have put the whole post in an uproar. After that guard duty was done with an empty pistol in our holster.

I had been an infantryman before I became an EOD specialist. During infantry training, we had *simulated* combat competitions between platoons. We were unable to use live ammunition, not even blanks. The powder in a blank, which causes the bang, is secured in the cartridge shell with a hard paper wad. The wad flies out of the barrel fast and really hurts if it hits bare skin. So, we would yell "bang, bang" at the opposing company, akin to kids playing.

Brow
inkstains.com

So, while walking guard duty in the EOD school building, I suppose, with my infantry training and my empty pistol, I should have been ready to yell "bang, bang" at any intruder...

The Canoe Trip

I had a couple of good friends when I was in EOD training. Binder, you've already met. There was also a fellow named Parch, Bill Parch. He was as much of a screwball as I was.

One night, he suggested canoeing on the river.

"First," I told him, "we don't have a canoe—and second, the river's over two miles away."

"No problem; we can borrow Franklin's car, and we can find a canoe when we get to the river. Somebody's got to have one over there."

Both being nuts, we "borrowed" Franklin's car for a couple of hours (he loaned it to us for five bucks) and Parch drove us over to the river. He parked underneath some willows behind a barn, and we walked down to the water.

Sure enough, there were some canoes pulled up on the bank, upside down. We took the paddles out from underneath

Brour
inkstains.com

one, flipped the canoe over, and slid it into the water. We paddled out a ways until we caught the current and floated downstream for a while. Parch said that we should have brought fishing gear or found some in the barn we had parked behind. He was even nuttier than I was. Maybe he expected us to find a shovel and dig for worms, too.

We were out there for a half-hour or so, slowly drifting, when I suggested that we better think about paddling back before we got too far downstream. Parch agreed.

I guess the flow had been a bit stronger than we had realized. It was tough going back up against the current. We didn't say much on the way back. It took too much effort just to paddle. One thing we did talk a little about was our longing for an outboard motor.

It took us more than two hours until we spotted the car parked behind the barn, and by then both of us were exhausted and our arms ached. We both also had blisters on our hands, which for me made driving back to base a chore.

We left the canoe on the bank as we had found it, with the paddles underneath, and hotfooted it back to the car as quietly as we could. Then we drove back to the base. We never tried canoeing again.

The Girl

Another time, I rented a car from Franklin to go to a nearby city on a three-day pass (Friday afternoon through Sunday afternoon), and I damaged the car. I was an inexperienced driver and was going too fast approaching an intersection with a traffic light. The light turned red sooner than expected. Slamming on the brakes, I slid half sideways and broke a tie rod. It was late in the day, early evening on a Friday in fact, but I was fortunate that the police towed me to an all-night repair shop.

I not only had to pay for the repair to the tie rod, but also had to pay for the tow and a hotel room—all at city prices. I was one unhappy fellow.

The next day, after picking up the car from the repair shop, I decided to do some sightseeing. I drove around the city for a while, exploring, and ended up at a park with a small lake. I spent some time watching the ducks in the pond, but they left me alone since I had nothing to feed them. A pretty girl came along, feeding the ducks bread. She asked me if I would like some of her bread, and I said, "Yes, thanks." After we were done feeding the ducks, I asked her if she would like to have lunch with me. She agreed and suggested a restaurant close by.

While we were eating and talking, I mentioned that I was from New York. She said that she was too and asked if I would like to go to a party with her that night. It sounded like a great idea, and we spent the rest of the afternoon together in the park, talking until evening about our families and the schools we had gone to. We were talking about where we lived and what our neighborhoods were like when we decided to eat. We returned to the restaurant for supper, and to my surprise, she insisted it was her turn to pay. I didn't argue. What a lucky fellow I was!

After supper, we got into our cars. Mine was practically on the other side of the park from hers, but we worked it out. I followed her on the way to the party. Then the disaster happened. We were on the highway, with her driving two cars ahead of me, and I swung out to pass the car between us. Suddenly, she took an offramp! There was no way I could possibly have made the lane change. Boy, oh, boy, did that put me in the dumps!

I considered getting off the highway at the next exit and going back to look for her, but then I thought that she probably thought I had done it on purpose. I drove back to the base, paid Franklin for the car rental, and went to bed a very unhappy guy.

The Gunnery Sergeant

After that episode, I was low on funds and realized that I hadn't been paid for a while. I sorely needed cash so I could buy snacks, go to town for the movies, rent Franklin's car and, of course, buy beer! So, I went to the school commandant's secretary, a marine gunnery sergeant, and asked him about it. He looked in his files and said that as far as he was concerned, I didn't even exist.

I told him I had an order sending me to the school from my previous duty station, which was the Chemical Weapons School as a prelude to EOD training. I had the actual paper order in with my stuff back at the barracks. He told me to get it and bring it to him, sending me with two sailors as an escort to make sure I didn't run away, I guess.

When I returned with the order, I was ushered into the commandant's office where he had been on the phone with the Chemical Weapons School. He told me that, according

inkstains.com

to the Army's records, I was AWOL (Absent Without Leave) since the school claimed it had no record of the order I had mentioned.

I was instructed to sit down for what seemed like the longest time in the gunnery sergeant's room, with the two sailors flanking me on either side. It was probably only a half-hour or so but it felt like half the day until the commandant came out of his office and motioned for me to come in.

I did, and he told me that the Chemical Weapons School had found their copy of my orders. He smiled and said, "If that's how the Army does things, I'm glad I'm a Marine." I asked the gunnery sergeant where I could go to get paid. He asked if I knew the location of the paymaster's office, I replied that I didn't and he provided me with directions. When I arrived at that office, the staff were very polite. It turned out that the gunnery sergeant had called and had gotten everything straightened out.

I admit that, for a while earlier, I had been a bit worried.

The Lieutenant

Here's another story about infantry training:

We had a "village" consisting of huts made of palmetto fronds that turned yellow after a while, so we had to go out in the fields and cut fresh fronds. This was not a pleasant job, but "orders are orders," as they say. That was the least of our village troubles.

Around the fake village was a ring of foxholes that some poor soldiers before us had dug, and we had to keep those from filling in, too. Sometimes the Army is so much fun.

One evening, the First Sergeant who oversaw most of our training had our platoon, all forty of us, form up in the company street. He told us that he hoped we had done a good job on the foxholes since we would be using them that night to defend the village against an attack from another platoon in our company. Our company's lieutenant would be evaluating the two teams from the village.

So, we took our positions around the village with un-loaded rifles and all our gear, including backpacks and extra empty ammunition magazines, I guess in case we needed to say "bang, bang" a lot, since I assume we carried "bang, bangs" in our ammunition magazines instead of bullets, and waited for the attack. And then it started to rain.

In situations like that, the troops take turns sleeping with the guys who are in alternating foxholes next to them who are awake.

Don't you believe it. That's what they were *supposed* to do. The "buddies" of mine on both sides of me fell asleep when they weren't supposed to, when it was my turn to sleep. That's the main reason I volunteered for Explosive Ordnance Disposal. It was safer.

Meanwhile, the rain was collecting in the bottoms of the foxholes, and we put up our ponchos over us on sticks to keep it off. Of course, the water just puddled in the middles of the ponchos until they became too heavy, and then everything overhead collapsed down on us all at once.

That's when the other team attacked, screaming and yelling "bang, bang" as they rushed through our line, between the foxholes, into the village. They kidnapped our lieutenant and carried him away, screaming into the night.

The next day, as a ransom for the lieutenant—which we were perfectly willing to forgo, letting them keep him forever—we had to clean their rain-soaked, mud-encrusted, rusty rifles, along with our own, which were in no better shape.

inkstains.com

Rest in Pieces

There was a medium-sized town about a half-hour north of our EOD detachment where, one early morning, the staff at a funeral home found the back door broken into.

They immediately called the police department, of course, and searched the business to see what had been stolen. What they discovered surprised them: nothing was missing. Then, while they were looking through the visitation (or viewing) room they noticed that the casket being displayed—with the preserved body ready for family and friends to view that morning—was improperly closed.

It held the body of a man with misshapen legs. The casket had a split lid with an open head panel, displaying the top half of his body. His lower torso and legs were to be covered by the closed-foot panel during the viewing. In the early morning, before the business opened, both sections of the lid should have been closed, and the foot panel screwed tight, as it would never be opened again.

One of the staff noticed a loosened screw on the foot panel. That made the funeral director wonder if the body had been tampered with below the waist. They unscrewed the lower half of the lid and lifted it off. That's when they got their second surprise of the morning: laid across the legs of the body was a bundle of four sticks of dynamite, taped together, with a blasting cap, wires, an alarm clock, and a battery.

The bomb, as we discovered later, was powerful enough to destroy not only the room, but also the whole building.

I won't describe it any more than what I already have because I don't want anyone reading this to know how to make one of these devices.

By this time, the police had arrived and instructed them to evacuate the building, directing them to wait at the end of the block.

That's when EOD received the call, this one *from* the police department.

Our clerk, John, answered it but quickly passed the phone to the captain. The captain listened for a minute, asked a couple of pertinent questions, informed them that we were on our way, and instructed John to arrange for a police escort to meet us at the post's gate. Then, he briefed us on the bare bones of the story while John was in the process of calling the State Police.

I loaded the toolbox into the back of the two-and-a-half-ton truck, along with half a dozen sandbags. First Sergeant Hemmings and I were next up on the duty list, but Captain Davis also came along with us.

We hopped into the truck's cab, spacious enough for three, with Hemmings at the wheel. We then drove through the base towards the gate that opened onto the state highway.

There were no State Police cars in sight, but after what felt like a minute (a looong minute), one finally arrived, roof lights flashing. Pulling up next to First Sergeant Hemmings' driver's door, the trooper stated that she knew where we were going and activated her siren to accompany the flashing roof lights. First Sergeant Hemmings, who already had the headlights and four-way flashers on, shifted the truck into gear and followed the trooper.

The trip, at ten miles an hour over the posted speed limit, didn't take long. Arriving a few minutes before nine o'clock, we found the street blocked off from end to end by police cars and firetrucks. Navigating around them, we parked in front of the building. As I retrieved the toolbox out of the back of our truck, a policeman brought us in through the front door. The viewing room, located to the right off of a short hallway, had a card next to the door indicating the deceased's name and viewing time: Paul Johnson, 11 A.M.

Captain Davis introduced us to the police lieutenant and sergeant, who were waiting in the viewing room, and asked them if anyone had touched anything. The lieutenant replied, "No, we waited for you guys." The captain then told the lieutenant to make sure that the area for a block around the funeral parlor had been evacuated, and the lieutenant told him it had been since the police had arrived more than an hour and a half before. The police lieutenant said that he'd like to stay for the disarmament procedure, and Captain Davis said he could. The police sergeant left the building and Captain Davis gave him time to get safely away.

First Sergeant Hemmings asked the captain, "Possible tremble switch, sir?"

"Not likely," Captain Davis replied. "He didn't want to kill us or the police; he wanted to kill the family who came to view the deceased."

"How did you know that?" the police lieutenant asked.

"If the bomber wanted to kill you or us, he would have used a different kind of fuse instead of a clock. This thing is set to go off at 11:15. The room should have been filled with people by then, and when the device exploded, it would have destroyed the whole building and everyone in it, including late arrivals."

"Probably a will dispute," the lieutenant volunteered.

"That's a possibility," the captain said, smiling.

I took the camera from the toolbox and snapped a dozen pictures of the room and its contents, including the open casket and the device within. Captain Davis examined the device and asked for the small wire cutters, which I handed to him from the toolbox. He asked First Sergeant Hemmings to hold

Brawz
inkstains.com

one of the wires attached to the battery to prevent it from falling into the casket. After cutting that wire, he then grasped the other wire connected to the battery and cut it as well, while I continued to take pictures of what he was doing.

Captain Davis returned the cutters to me and took hold of the wire that Hemmings had held. Holding the battery by the two cut-off wires, he placed it into a plastic bag I gave him from the toolbox. He gave the bag to the police lieutenant since the battery could potentially bear fingerprint evidence.

"So that's it, then?" the lieutenant asked, dumbfounded. "Snip, snip, and it's all over?"

"Just about," the captain replied, carefully removing the blasting cap from the sticks of dynamite. "But don't think they're all this simple," he said, grinning.

First Sergeant Hemmings took a pair of rubber gloves out of the toolbox, put them on to avoid smearing any fingerprints on the cap's body, and twisted together the two wires coming out of it to prevent them from accidently picking up any static electricity. He was careful not to touch the shiny metal of the cap's body.

He placed the cap into a different plastic bag that I gave him and handed the bag to the police lieutenant. "More possible fingerprint evidence, sir," he said. "Just be careful; blasting caps are small, but they're nasty."

The captain offered to dispose of the dynamite, but the police lieutenant turned his offer down, stating that they could take care of it just fine.

Captain Davis told the police lieutenant that the police could allow people in the area back into their homes, that the bomb was disarmed, and the lieutenant gave the appropriate order over his radio. He then went out to his car and returned with his briefcase, which he took into the funeral home's office, with Captain Davis following him.

"The job's not over 'til the paperwork's done, I guess," remarked First Sergeant Hemmings, and the two of us went into the small kitchen to get coffee.

We drank our coffee sitting at the small table and two chairs that took up most of the space in the small room. After about twenty minutes, the captain came and got us. We shook hands all around, and then we left. On the way out, we noticed that the police department had taken away the dynamite. I guess they wanted it for evidence.

Outside, newspaper and TV reporters and photographers surrounded us. The captain said a few innocuous words, the police lieutenant announced that it was all over, and we all had our pictures taken on the way to the truck.

The trip home was, thankfully, uneventful.

BUT, a story about our visit and a photo of us coming out of the building were in the newspaper the next day, so it all worked out okay in a couple of ways!

www.ingramcontent.com/pod-product-compliance
Lightning Source LLC
Chambersburg PA
CBHW061344140726
47997CB00003B/1044